BERT HARRIS OF THE POLY

Front page of Le Vélodrôle, *June 24, 1894*

DICK SWANN

Bert Harris of The Poly

VANCE HARVEY PUBLISHING
LEICESTER

First Edition 1964
Printed by Syston Printing Co, Syston, Leicester

Second Edition 1973
© Dick Swann 1964

Printed in England

This edition was published by Vance Harvey Publishing,
29 Horsefair Street, Leicester, England
Printed by Daedalus Press, Stoke Ferry, King's Lynn, Norfolk
Bound by Adams and Harrison Ltd, Biggleswade, Bedfordshire

CONTENTS

Chapter		Page
	FOREWORD	7
	INTRODUCTON	8
	AUTHOR'S NOTE	10
1	A LEICESTER GHOST	11
2	BERT ARRIVES IN LEICESTER	13
3	A NEW ERA	17
4	BUSY YEARS	26
5	FAMILY TROUBLES	35
6	PROFESSIONAL!	42
7	DISASTER	45
8	'HARRIS YEAR'	49
9	PREMONITION	53
10	LINKS	59
11	COMMENTS	63
	EPILOGUE	67
	APPENDIX	68

ILLUSTRATIONS

(Frontispiece)
The front page of *Le Vélodrôle,* June 1894

(between pp 38 and 39)
Winning at Aston Track, Easter 1897
After winning the National Amateur Championship in 1891
Club Track Champion of the Polytechnic CC, 1893
British Professional Champion
Before his trip to Australia in 1895
The Harris Trophy
The twelve best path racers of 1891

FOREWORD

BY THE AUTHOR

I have been assured by some very keen and erudite cyclists, who have read my manuscript, that this is a 'good effort'. If it gives any pleasure to the reader, then I must point out the really wonderful help so unselfishly given me in my research into Harris's life, by my great friends, Alan Whitworth, Jack Woodford, Sid Mottram, and Wally Gray.

DICK SWANN

INTRODUCTION

BY A E ('Paddy') ROEBUCK, *Norwood Paragon C.C.*

Dick Swann is an old racing rival, a good friend, and a most knowledgeable cyclist. We raced (in rival teams) on the hot and dusty roads of Egypt years ago; Dick was a well-known writer even then, on cycling matters. His weekly contributions to *Cycling* and *Bicycle* were read with interest by cyclists the World over. When the War ended, Dick stayed on in Libya on the staff of the *Tripoli Times;* even having the impudence to win the Sprint Championship of Tripoli against the 'locals', on the steeply-banked 'Velodromo del Littorio' in Tripoli, in 1946.

Returning to 'Blighty', Dick was honoured by being made Chairman of the 'Service Cyclists' Reunion', sponsored by Sir Edmund Crane of 'Hercules', and held in London. In those well-remembered ten 'boom years' of cycle-sport, 1947 to 1957, Dick was manager of two famous bike-shops (Hetchin's and Freddie Grubb); was promoter of big meetings on Herne Hill, Paddington, Slough, Reading and Wolverton tracks; was a regular cycling news correspondent on a varied collection of journals, including *Cycling Gazette, Weekly Sporting Review, Speedway Gazette, Civil Service Sports Journal* (he was National Secretary and 25 miles Champion of the Civil Service Cycling Association); and even got some half-page articles on Cycling, into the ultra-conservative *Jewish Chronicle*!

Dick is known these days as a B.C.F. Judge, Starter, Committeeman, and Clerk-of-Course; in the past he won hundreds of prizes at distances ranging from 300 yards on the track, to 12 hours on the road. Perhaps Dick's most popular contribution to

INTRODUCTION

this Bike Game of ours, is his series of humorous 'tomtug' books – which have received high praise from such notable trackmen as Binch, Handley, Whitfield, Harrison and Barton. His *Junior Bike Rider* is a classic 'Beginner's Textbook' and is a measure of Dick's ability as a Coach; his coaching work includes 'bossing' the Herne Hill 'Nursery', the Paddington Track School, and the Polytechnic 'Nursery' ... sixteen years of actual practical coaching, as opposed to the 'paper Coaching' of some modern 'armchair experts'. Now comes Dick's first full-length essay as a Cycling Historian, and a fascinating slice of 'Victoriana' it is, too.

The Bert Harris story takes place in the absolute peak-period of cycle-racing history, when in place of the present-day worship of make-believe heroes of stage and screen, the Victorians bestowed their adulation on the athletic, real-life performers in those two great Victorian sports, Cycling and Boxing.

(The big-name Football Clubs were just being formed, but Football hadn't yet acquired the 'Pools', nor had it yet supplanted Christianity as the English Religion!).

At this time, also, Dick's grandfather was a well-known cycling personality, being Captain of the Newhaven C.C., a regular prizewinner, and proprietor of the 'Knight' concern in Newhaven, turning out a high-grade light racing cycle. Dick's wife and daughter are members of the old-established Leicestershire R.C., and I had great pleasure in meeting these two girls recently, while on tour in the Midlands. Dick's son also shows promise as a cyclist, having won a collection of trophies that include the 'Enfield Cup', 'Winter Cup', 'Hetchins Cup', 'Ward Bowl', 'Davies Cup', etc., etc., so the Swann tribe will continue to flourish for a while yet – and maybe Dick will give us more 'Nineties Stories' to follow 'Bert Harris'?

A E (PADDY) ROEBUCK

AUTHOR'S NOTE

Sadly I record the death of 'Paddy', only a few days after he so kindly wrote the above gracious Introduction.

Paddy's life was rich and varied, and took him around the World. He always rode a bike, whether his current home was in Turkey, Brazil or England. He 'lived' every minute of his life, and was a 100 per cent bikerider, having no time for motorised transport. His son, Arthur, is one of the Norwood Paragon's most promising junior roadmen, and has inherited Paddy's enthusiastic nature.

DICK SWANN

CHAPTER ONE

A LEICESTER GHOST

LEICESTER HAS MANY TRAGIC FIGURES in its history, but surely one of the most interesting ghosts that people this ancient city, is that of Albert Walter Allen Harris. Or, as he was more affectionately known in most of the civilised countries of the World, just 'Bert'.

Bert Harris, Champion Amateur Track Cyclist of England, later Champion Professional of England, was perhaps the greatest Sportsman in Leicestershire history; certainly he was its greatest Bike Rider. At his funeral in 1897, the town turned out 'in tens of thousands', to quote the *Leicester Daily Post*. 'The streets were crowded; such a funeral scene has never been equalled in Leicester', continued the same paper; 'at the Leicester Cemetery' (now known as the Welford Road Cemetery – author), 'hundreds of people filled every coign of vantage, while the Vicar of Holy Trinity read the service'.

The Leicester Weekly 'paper commented: 'No more eloquent tribute to the World-wide renown of the late Bert Harris could have been found than the remarkable way in which the people of Leicester turned out en masse to do honour at his funeral. The streets through which the cortege passed on its way from the late residence at No. 4, Portsmouth Road, to the cemetery – a distance of two miles – were simply thronged with vast crowds of people, who turned out to demonstrate their sympathy with one who represented all that was highest in the world of athletics, and who was typical of the best in English sport'.

Yet how many people – even members of present-day cycling

clubs – in Leicester, have even heard of Harris? As they walk or ride up University Road (in Harris's time it was known as Victoria Road), they pass within a few feet of his grave – a monument subscribed for by 'the Cyclists of England', with a copper bust-in-relief of this tragic young man, and the following inscription as an epitaph:

> 'In Affectionate Memory of
>
> ALBERT WALTER ALLEN HARRIS,
>
> this memorial stone is erected by the
> Cyclists of England,
> as a token of the sincere respect and esteem in which he was held by Wheelmen the World over. He was ever a fair and honourable rider and sportsman and his lamented death cut off in his prime one of the brightest and most genial spirits of Cycledom. He fell on the racing path at Aston on Easter Monday, 1897, and succumbed to his injuries at the General Hospital, Birmingham, April 21st, 1897,
>
> aged 24 years'.

A curious feature is the incorrect age given on the stone, as Harris was, in fact, just turned 23 at his death.

CHAPTER TWO

BERT ARRIVES IN LEICESTER

BERT WAS BORN IN BIRMINGHAM on 9th April, 1874, and had two sisters, Ethel and Louisa, and an elder brother. (The latter married and settled down in Birmingham in 1889).

Between 1880 and 1885, the Belgrave area of Leicester was being built up as part of the Second Industrial Expansion, and Harris senior, a Bookmaker by profession, moved with his family into one of the new houses in one of the new roads – No. 4, Portsmouth Road, connecting the Loughborough Road to the Melton Road.

He later opened a Gunsmith's shop near the junction of these two roads. He was a well-known figure at local Sporting events, including Cycle-race meets, and the Horse-racing meetings held in those days in Victoria Park.

The new Harris domicile was in handy proximity to the nationally-famous Belgrave Road Sports Grounds, the site of which is now covered by the giant B.U.S.M.C. factory.

The Belgrave Road Ground was the scene of hundreds of important Amateur and Professional Athletic and Cycling meetings, on the 3-laps-to-the-mile cinder track.

The last National Championships to be held there were the N.C.U. Mile and 25 miles events of 1881, both won by G. Lacy Hillier of the Stanley Bicycle Club on 16th July.

Lacy Hillier was later to become N.C.U. Senior Judge, and acted in his capacity of Judge for many of Bert's races in later years.

In 1878 a new 3-laps-to-the-mile cinder track had been laid in the open space at Grace Road, known as the Aylestone Road Recreation Grounds.

(This is now the Leicestershire Cricket Club ground).

The 'Infirmary Sports' in aid of Leicester's Infirmary (previously known as the Fever Hospital), were run off annually on the new Aylestone Road grounds, and Bert Harris actually began his cycling career in Schoolboy Races on this track.

After the 1914-18 War, the ground was still used for cycling meetings, but on a grass-track in the centre, 4-laps-to-the-mile. These Sports continued until the late 1920's, when the Infirmary Sports were discontinued.

(The present-day Leicester Track League uses the grass-track in the Saffron-Lane area).

In Harris's time, the Aylstone Road track was firm, hard and beautifully rolled; but not quite so fast as the better-designed and smaller circuits such as Paddington (London), on which Bert was later to gain some satisfying victories.

Big professional matches were held at the Aylestone Road grounds, and one sample advertised locally for September, 1888 (in the Infirmary Sports programme), gives details of a match between Fred Wood, a Leicester man who belonged to the Brixton (London) club, and Ralph Temple of America, for a purse of £50, which Temple won. Temple was one of America's best, while Wood had taken National Championships in 1888, on both bicycle and tricycle, in Newcastle and Coventry respectively.

The first National Championship to be held on the Aylestone Road ground was the '25' on July 25th, 1885, when R H English won in 1 hour, 20 minutes, 13 seconds, before a crowd of 14,000 people. Bob English was a member of the North Shields club, and the sight of the big Newcastle man, with his flaming red jockey-cap, thrashing his rivals on the old 'High' bicycles, was a great thrill to Bert and his close school chum, Will Jordan, who had been taken along by Harris senior – who had a 'professional' interest in the racing.

Will Jordan lived at 68, Welford Road (on the corner of James Street), and the two boys attended Holy Trinity Church and School together; remaining close friends until Bert's untimely death. Will was a frequent visitor to No. 4, Portsmouth Road, where the two boys would peruse Harris senior's back-numbers of *Bicycling News* and argue over the respective merits of the Oxford and Cambridge bicycle racers (Inter-University races began in 1874, and ceased on the outbreak of the Boer War; many famous riders, including Whatton, Weir, Swann, Keith-Falconer and Gatehouse, first came into prominence via the inter-University cycle matches).

Bert was encouraged by his father to take up cycling; started on a 'New Rapid', with solid tyres and flat handlebar, and began in Schoolboy events in 1888, at 14 years of age.

Being a tiny lad (even as a man he never topped 5ft. 2ins.), with a frail appearance, his perky little face looking out merrily from under his beribboned school 'boater', raised some smiles and won the hearts of the female spectators. (Description vide *Leicester Post*). As late as 1892, when Harris was 18, he was 'very boyish-looking' according to a Poly C.C. contemporary of his, A E Davies.

In the early days of bike-racing, headgear was varied, the riders using jockey-caps, 'boaters', bobcaps or deer-stalkers, as took their fancy. Any amusement his rivals may have felt, however, was quickly dispelled in the next couple of years. In 1890, at 16 years old, he took 3rd prize in the Open 880 yards handicap at the Infirmary Sports, in June.

Bert's schooldays hero, Bob English, had won the National 1-mile Professional Championship in April, on the same track, Aylestone Road.

In 1891 at the Infirmary meeting Bert was on virtual scratch, riding from the very short mark of 10 yards in the 880, and 20 yards in the Mile. He collected 2nd in the 880, and 3rd in the Mile. The *Leicester Post* of 30th June, 1891, commented: 'Harris rode magnificently. He was the hero of the afternoon, the youthful rider setting a great pace on his machine, and splendidly maintaining his reputation as one of the very fastest riders in England today'.

Harris senior, of course, had quite a 'professional interest' in the Belgrave Road and Aylestone Road cycling meets, and Mr

Allcroft of Trinity Hospital, reminiscing in 1962, says, 'I well remember old Harris the bookie, calling "six to four my son Bert!"' (Betting was a natural adjunct to trackmeets in those days). Mr Allcroft lived in a house in Hawkesbury Road (rent 5/- weekly!) overlooking the Aylestone Road grounds, and recalls Bert Harris in his red jersey as a 'very spectacular rider'.

He was soon to be wearing a more famous jersey, as a Poly member and National Champion.

CHAPTER THREE

A NEW ERA

BERT HARRIS, OF COURSE, HAD ENTERED the Bike Game at the end of the old 'High Bicycle' era, and at the beginning of the low-built 'Safety Bicycle' era. The 1890-1 period also saw the swift end of the solid tyre for racing purposes, and the introduction of the new 'pudding tyres' as pneumatics were (at first) derisively termed. Dunlop patented his tyre on 23rd July, 1888, but the actual invention had been made in 1845 by Thompson, who lacked the bicycle to put it to practical test. Edlin and Sinclair, Belfast, cycle makers, built bicycles for Dunlop, to give clearance for the wider pneumatics; it must be remembered that the bicycle of 1888 had forks and chainstays designed to accommodate thin solid 'bootlace' tyres; these had to be re-designed to take a two-inch 'pudding', which meant new forgings for crown and bracket.

The majority of big makers had large stocks of lugs, brackets, etc., suitable for solid-tyred machines, and were against the new tyre on principle. W Hume, Belfast Cruisers, was the first man to race on Dunlops. Hume had been a successful High Bicycle trackman, and his last rides on the High Bicycle had netted 4 prizes at Ulster during Easter, 1888. Then a bad crash decided him to retire; then came the offer of a free 'Edlin' racing safety, with 'Dunlop' pneumatics. On this he took four 'firsts' at Queen's College Sports, Belfast, on 18th May, 1889, with a gear of 62in., 30in. rear wheel and 28in. front. Hume's next appearance was at Liverpool Police Sports on 20th July, 1889, winning the one and three miles handicaps from 130 and 310 yards marks respectively. The hoots of laughter which greeted the 'Humatic', 'cartwheel', 'steamroller', pudding wheels', as spectators variously termed the 'old Irish home-made bicycle', were capped by the handicapper's comment: 'If I'd known you were going to ride a machine like that, I'd have put you on a longer mark!'.

He changed his mind after the racing.

The Edlin-Dunlop was then exhibited in the shop window of Baker, Cycle Agent, of Lime Street, Liverpool; and the resulting crowd of sightseers caused obstruction and had to be moved by the police.

This success prompted the great Irish rider, R J Mecredy of the Dublin University Bicycle Club (he was Editor of the *Irish Cyclist*), to invade England in search of Championships in 1890. Mecredy collected the Mile, 5 miles, '25', and '50' N.C.U. National titles, all on the Paddington track in London, between July 12th and August 13th, 1890.

The following year the Irish contingent came over again, led by Arthur du Cros; but by this time the English trackmen had mastered the peculiarities of the pneumatic tyres, and there was 'nothing doing' for the sons of Erin. While in England, the Irish boys were the guests of the Poly club, and George Apsey, a Poly boy of the time, reminiscing in 1962 at the age of 91 says: 'I remember du Cros and the Irish boys coming down to the Poly clubroom; a nice lot of chaps they were'. In June, 1891, the Irish contingent raced a match against the Poly at Paddington track; the Poly winning fairly easily. On 18th July, Harris, on his 'Dunlops', collected the N.C.U. National 5 miles Championship on the Bristol track. But to continue with the story of the Big Change. Not only had the pneumatic 'come in', but also the 'Safety', or Low Bicycle, with chain drive. This had been invented by J K Starley in 1888, and curiously enough was more popular in America, to start with.

(Starley became one of the first 'Bicycle Millionaires', Managing Director of the 'Rover' Cycle and Motor Company, and a pioneer of the motor car and motor cycle trades. He was a member of the Midland C. & A.C. Starley inaugurated the annual Inter-Clubrun with the Poly in 1898; this developed into an annual race, the latest winner (1963) being Poly Midland

Section rider Bob Hughes. This annual event is promoted alternately by the Poly and the M.C.A.C.).

In August, 1888, S G Whittaker knocked off World's Records at 5 miles (13–33 2/5) and 1 hour (21m. 126yds.), on one of Starley's 'Rover' machines. This cooked the goose of the High Bicycle, and with the addition of the pneumatic tyre, the Big Change was on. From 1878 (in which year the first National Championships were held, and in which year also the Polytechnic C.C. and the Cyclist's Touring Club were both founded), until 1888, the High Bicycle, jocularly re-named 'penny-farthing' by the Penny Press of the 1920's, had been the fastest type of cycle available. And, in fact, some riders, including the great Osmond, were still racing on High machines against Safeties, right up to 1890. Then, owing to the danger of mixed fields, the two types were confined to separate races. To differentiate, the High Bicycle was referred to as the 'Ordinary' cycle, and the new type referred to as the 'Safety'.

It took some little time for the Ordinary to die out, as the old school of riders, notably Lacy Hillier, Osmond, and Johnny Adams, obstinately refused to believe that the safety was better or faster. For a little while, the Ordinary, fitted with pneumatics, held its own; and as late as 1890, the 1 mile handicap (Ordinary), was won in a faster time than the 1 mile handicap (Safety) at Paddington. This was in a special race meeting promoted by Lord Randolph Churchill and Dr E B Turner, a Vice-President of the Poly club, at the Paddington track on 9th July, 1890. The events were the 'Royal Handicaps', with the Prince and Princess of Wales as interested guests of honour, at their first cycle-race meeting. Naturally, it rained; but the Royal party, in a covered stand inside the running track opposite the Finish, were quite happy. The Tricycle race was won by Oxford University B.C. man Lewis Stroud in 2m. 42 1/5 s. (The limit man, A J Watson, Catford C.C., was last. Watson later joined the Poly and reached World class).

The Safety race was won in 2m. 33 3/5 s. by W Price, Poly, off 30 yards. The track was, to quote a reporter of the time, 'rather holding' – not surprising, considering the weather, and the clay-cum-cinders surface of the track! Arthur du Cros, an Irish visitor, off 20yds., was 2nd, and G L Morris, Poly, off 45yds. 3rd.

Ernie Leitch, Poly, the scratchman, was last.

The fastest time of the day was in the Ordinary race, won by giant Fred Osmond (Brixton) in 2 mins. 31 4/5 secs. W Bardsley of the Hounslow B.C., off 60 yards, was unplaced. Bardsley later joined the Poly, and like A J Watson, won National Championships and turned 'pro'. Nevertheless, the Ordinary was doomed. The High Bicycle champions were all giants of over 6 foot; Adams, English, Osmond, Wood, Lambley and Cortis being typical examples. The reason being obvious – the tall man could bestride a larger diameter wheel and consequently a bigger gear. The advent of the chain-driven Safety – with the size of gear depending not on the diameter of the wheel, but on the combination of sprocket and chainwheel fitted – plus the advent of the pneumatic tyre – gave the small man an equal chance with the tall fellow.

In fact, taking into consideration the soft and yielding surfaces of the tracks of the time, ranging from grass, cinders and clay, to brickdust, gravel or just hard-rammed earth(!), the small man, who didn't sink in so deeply, actually had an advantage over the bigger, more heavily-built rider.

Bert Harris was the first of the Good Little 'Uns, coming into the game at just the right moment, with cycle design, track surfaces and fat pneumatics, combining with his lightweight and nippy pedalling action, to completely change the Cycling Scene. He was followed by a string of 'great little men', including Alec Watson, Ernie Leitch, J. W. Stocks, Jimmy Michael, the Lintons and many others.

One of Bert's early victories was a win over the above-mentioned Johnny Adams (a National Champion of 1887 and 1888).

This was at Long Eaton in July, 1892. Bert also beat Osmond (Manchester, July 1892), and Lambley (who later joined the Poly), and Wood. Bert never met English or Cortis in competition. Cortis emigrated to Australia in the early 1880's, and Bob English retired in 1887.

A NEW ERA

Machines, equipment and positions were changing rapidly week by week, in the early 'nineties and it was undoubtedly 'the liveliest period in the history of cycling', as Reg Wellbye puts it.

The first Safety riders adopted positions similar to that they'd used on their High bicycles; body upright, legs fully extended, saddle way back from the pedals, and handlebar grips level with a point midway along the top-tube. Gradually the grips were brought forward, the saddle also; the body inclining with them; until by 1896 the 'extended stem' was 'in', angles were steepened, and performances improved as the back muscles were brought into use, with new, almost 'modern' positions.

Writing in 1920, S A Mussabini (a famous Poly Coach of the 'nineties) said : 'The boom of the 'nineties can't be forgotten. In a very few days after the first practical racing demonstrations of the pneumatic's capabilities, the solid rubber tyre was completely out of date. What a boom it was! The Midlands manufacturing towns were working night and day to satisfy public demand and make bundles of money for the company promoters, who became known as "Bicycle Millionaires". When the cycling boom was at its highest the Dunlop people added to the attractions of the cycle racetracks by building long machines capable of seating three, four, five, six, and eight riders, whose simultaneous leg-drive was the counterpart of a racing boat's crew. These pacing crews, known as triplets, quads, quints, sextets and octets, made a fine sight as they swung up the straight and took the bends with their "singles" tucked in, close up. Pacing nowadays is performed by motor cycles – much more noisily, and far less spectacularly'.

The first tracks were flagged-out grass circuits, similar to the grasstracks used nowadays at country Fetes and Flower Shows. Some of the best-known of Harris's day were the Oval, Watford, Wembley, Sydenham, Ravensbourne, Headingley, etc. Some grasstrack promotions, such as Watford, Hertford and Ravensbourne, are still put on as regular annual meetings to this day! Later tracks were of clay or coaldust; watered, rolled and rammed down hard. The glimmerings of scientific track-laying were evident when G Lacy Hillier wrote in 1888 :

'Special points about laying a cycle-track are as follows:
1 It must be as level as possible.
2 It must be wide – not less than 18 feet.
3 It must be hard, with a solid basis; soft running tracks are not suitable for cycling.
4 The corners must be banked, 5 feet or more, to assist the cyclist to overcome centrifugal force generated by his speed along the straights.

Tracks are made of cinder alone; of cinder and burnt clay; of gravel; of clay; or combinations of these. The attendant must watch and nurse his path assiduously'.

Made-up tracks (with cinder, shale or gravel surfaces) used by Bert Harris in his early racing days, included the following:

Alexandra Palace, London (3 laps to Mile).
Aylestone Road, Leicester (3 laps to Mile).
Aston Lower Grounds, Birmingham (4 laps to Mile).
Belgrave Road, Leicester (3 laps to Mile).
Bow Grounds, London (4 laps to Mile).
Balham, London (4 laps to Mile).
Coventry (4 laps to Mile).
Cambridge (4 laps to Mile).
County Grounds, Bristol (3 laps to Mile).
Crystal Palace, Sydenham (3 laps to Mile).
Fallowfield ($3\frac{1}{2}$ laps to Mile).
High Beech, Essex (4 laps to Mile).
Herne Hill, London ($3\frac{1}{2}$ laps to Mile).
Hampden Park, Glasgow (4 laps to Mile).
Hanson Lane, Halifax ($3\frac{1}{2}$ laps to Mile).
Jarrow, Newcastle-on-Tyne (4 laps to Mile).
Kensal Rise (London) (3 laps to Mile).
Long Eaton, Notts. ($2\frac{1}{2}$ laps to Mile).
Lillie Bridge, London (4 laps to Mile).
North Durham, Newcastle-on-Tyne (3 laps to Mile).
North Shields, Newcastle-on-Tyne ($3\frac{1}{2}$ laps to Mile).
Oxford Track (3 laps to Mile).
Paddington, London ($3\frac{1}{2}$ laps to Mile).

A NEW ERA

Paignton Track (4 laps to Mile).
Preston Park, Brighton (3 laps to Mile).
Reading, Berkshire (3½ laps to Mile).
Sheen, London (3 laps to Mile).
Stamford Bridge, London (3 laps to Mile).
Surbiton, Surrey (3 laps to Mile).
Sophia Gardens, Cardiff (4 laps to Mile).
Taunton Athletic Grounds (3 laps to Mile).
Tufnell Park (4 laps to Mile).
Torquay Track (4 laps to Mile).
Weston-super-Mare (3½ laps to Mile).
Worsley Track, Grimsby (4 laps to Mile).

In Bert's later racing days, the best-known and fastest cement tracks were all in the London district, and included the following:

Catford (3½ laps to Mile).
Crystal Palace (3 laps to Mile).
Canning Town (3½ laps to Mile).
Herne Hill (3½ laps to Mile).
Kensal Rise (3 laps to Mile).
Paddington (3½ laps to Mile).
Putney (4½ laps to Mile).
St. Albans (4 laps to Mile).
Wood Green (3½ laps to Mile).

At one time, Herne Hill was wood-surfaced (1893); the two best-known British wood-surfaced tracks were both indoor circuits – Olympia (9 laps to Mile) and the Westminster Acquarium (10 laps to Mile) – both in London.

Harry Woolcott, Paddington Bicycle Club trackman who was a star of the Putney Velodrome meetings, speaking in 1936 to the author, said: 'This track was well sheltered, and some wonderful meetings were put on there. Harry Carter of the Poly won a great 24-hours invitation contest on this track. The groundsman was W G George, a famous professional runner, who had won a challenge Mile race against W Cummings, before 20,000 spectators at the famous red ballast ¼ mile Lillie Bridge track, putting up a World Record of 4 mins., 12 3/5 secs.'.

In Harris's day, and in fact up until the Kaiser's War, the N.C.U. National and Centre Championships were open to all-comers. The National titles continued to be open to all-comers until 1935, when the Sprint Championship went to German Toni Merkens; in 1936 the National titles were confined to English nationals, and Poly rider Charlie Helps won the Sprint.

The Amateur Athletic Association still allow foreigners to compete for their titles nowadays; and in certain cases, men with residential qualifications may still compete for B.C.F. National Championships – e.g., Australian Brian Dew riding in the 1963 Sprint Championship.

The Centre (now known as 'Division') Championships of the N.C.U. (now the B.C.F.) have been for many years open to (A.) Riders residing in the Centre; and (B.) Members of clubs affiliated to the Centre. Thus, for instance, while Poly Midland Section riders Johnson, Green, and McCarthy, chose to win their B.C.F. medals in Midlands Divisions in 1962-3, on the other hand Poly Midlands Section riders Burns, Archer and Whitfield, preferred to take their B.C.F. medals in London Division Championships in 1962-3. It is interesting to note that Poly boy Tourunnen, a clubmate contemporary of Harris, and a naturalised Englishman, took 3 National titles of Finland. The quality of the English National Champions of those days, is highlighted by the fact that not only did they have to overcome the best of their own countrymen – they also had to defeat such foreign opposition as Zimmerman, Protin, Sanger, Mecredy, and scores of others. Thus the true worth of Harris, Watson, Synyer, Lambley, Cherry, Payne, Ingram, and other Poly National Champions of the 1890's, can be appreciated.

The first National Champion of England was Arthur Markham, who won England's first official Bicycle Race on a track marked out at the back of the old 'Welsh Harp' public house at Hendon. (The Welsh Harp reservoir was built in Victorian times by altering the shape of a natural lake). Markham later opened a bicycle shop in Edgware Road, Kilburn, not far from the site of Paddington track. By the 1890's, however, cycle-racing had

A NEW ERA

become fully organised, with its own governing body, a strong Press, and full Trade backing.

Until the formation of the Bicycle Union (later renamed the National Cyclist's Union, and later still to become the B.C.F.) in 1878, the National (and World's!) Championships were arranged by professional promoters, cycle-manufacturers, Athletic Clubs, bookies (nowadays known as 'Turf Accountants'), and pub-managers. (E G, the 'Molineux Arms' at Wolverhampton, the 'Welsh Harp' at Hendon, etc.). Fred Wood of Leicester won several National pro. titles under these conditions. In 1876 one athletic journal sneered at the new sport, commenting on the mentality of the 'twelve thousand people who went to watch two men ride a mile at Wolverhampton'.

H O Duncan, an Englishman residing in Paris and working there as (among other things) Agent for Rudge Cycles, came over to Leicester in 1881 to win the 'World's Professional Bicycling Championship' on the Belgrave Road track. Duncan is pictured in sporting journals of the time, wearing his Championship Belt, a huge affair of many silver shields and medallions, modelled on the boxing title belts.

Duncan, English, Keen, Wood, Cooper and the rest of the ace pro. riders, were ignored by the N.C.U., which concerned itself solely with 'gentleman amateurs'. The pro. rider wasn't considered a gentleman, or even a genuine performer. Nevertheless, their times and performances were fully checked and authenticated by the most eagle-eyed judges of all – the betting public! When, in 1894, the N.C.U. decided that professionals were, after all, worthy of consideration, the sport of cycling took a further upward leap in popularity and respectability. Result – the Boom Years of 1895 to 1899. Bert Harris's National Pro. title was of course, this first N.C.U. pro. promotion. Incidentally, what a sad commentary on present-day Leicester, with no proper track, when one reflects on its glorious past! Particularly when Birmingham, Derby, Nottingham, Kettering, Coventry, and other neighbouring towns all have properly-built hard-surfaced cycling tracks. And yet Leicester folk boast of their 'prosperous' city (which can't afford a cycle track!).

CHAPTER FOUR

BUSY YEARS

In 1891 Bert applied for membership of, and was considered good enough to be accepted by, the mighty Polytechnic C.C. – then, as now, the most famous track club in England. C W Schafer, a Poly man, who was proprietor of the Leicester Cycle Company, which turned out the famous 'Peregrine' racing cycles in Leicester, seconded Bert's application for membership. In 1891 Bert took his first National medal, winning the Amateur 5 miles Championship on the Ashley Down track at Bristol, a cinder circuit with 3-foot banking, 3 laps-to-the-mile. A visit to London in September netted him 1st place in the classic 1 mile 'Sydney Trophy' and 3rd in the equally classic 10 miles 'Surrey Cup' race, both held at the Kennington Oval grasstrack, and promoted by the Surrey B.C.

His last win of 1891 was a Trophy victory at Jarrow, late in September.

(The Railway Age was very handy to the Victorian bike-riders, who did more travelling than their modern counterparts).

Bert blossomed into a real all-rounder, and an indication of this is in his victories, which ranged in distance from 400 yards to 25 miles.

(Truly an instance of what Bill Fisher, the Barnet C.C's veteran track official, means when he refers to 'the typical Poly sprinter-stayer' – perpetuated in later years by Dave Ricketts, Don Burgess, Ian Alsop, Peter Robinson, and many others).

Bert made himself a favourite with the London crowds, in the

Surrey B.C's classic meets on Kennington Oval, now better known for Cricket.

These 'Surrey Meets' were held twice a year, in April and September; the two main events being the 'Sydney Trophy' over 1 mile, and the 'Surrey Cup' over 10 miles. Both were 50-guinea trophies.

Bert won the 'Surrey Cup' 3 times – in September, '92, April, 1893, and September, 1893, thus making it his own property. He also won the 'Sydney' three times – September, '91, September, '92, and April, '93. (The break for April, '92 was a victory for Arthur du Cros, with Lambley 2nd and Bert 3rd).

An indication of the standing of the 'Sydney Trophy' is in this comment by *The Hub* of 17th April, '97 : 'The holder of the Sydney Trophy may be said to be the short-distance champion of the year'.

While Bert was concentrating on grass-tracks in 1891, the famous Herne Hill track was being built, with Charlie Wilson as groundsman. Wilson, who died during the 1914-18 War, had this to say of Bert : 'The gamest little fighter I ever saw on the racing path'.

Around this time Bert was referred to in the cycling press and the Poly magazines at 'The Kid', once again drawing attention to his youthful appearance.

Bert started 1892 with a 'Bang'! taking 9 firsts and 2 seconds in 12 races at Eastertime, including a win over Arthur du Cros. The next big win was the 'Wolverhampton Shield', a massive and ornate silver trophy put up to Team competition. Bert led his Poly clubmates Alf Edwards and Alf Mole to a 1-2-3 victory, thus making sure of maximum points.

In 1892 the Poly adopted the now world-famous colours of 'dark-blue and cardinal red'; the blue vest carrying a red diamond on the back, a Poly badge on the chest, and red zig-zag trimming to neck and sleeves. There was talk, in 1892, of resurfacing Paddington track with cement. Amazing as it may seem now, there was controversy as to whether the new cement surface was faster than cinders! A new cement-surfaced track had been laid at Kensal Rise by the pioneer of cement tracks,

James Barden – whose son Charles was later to be a fellow-professional of Bert's. (James Barden later built the famous Putney Velodrome, a very steep and small track (4½ laps to the mile) on the Wimbledon side of Putney Bridge; and later building cement tracks in Denmark and Sweden).

The Kensal Rise track, near the modern Kensal Rise railway station, was less than 2 miles from Paddington; and the Poly, in common with other local clubs, tried out the new surface by promoting meetings there in 1892. That it proved slower than Paddington, was mainly the fault of its wide-open position at the top of a hill, subject to every wind that blew; also, the design (3 laps-to-the-mile) was inferior to Paddington; and the surface, laid in sections, tended to settle unevenly and thus 'tilt' the sections, with obvious results. When first built, only the inside part (10 feet wide) was cement-surfaced; the outer part remaining cinders. Later, the entire width was cemented. The *Poly C.C. Gazette* of May, 1893, refers to Kensal Rise as 'the Cement Track', thus emphasising its novelty. (Although later cement tracks such as Catford, Wood Green, Paddington, Putney, etc., were much better, as contractors grew more skilled in the use of the new material, and took more care over the foundations, it will be noticed that even on modern cement tracks such as Slough, that the sections are still imperfectly joined, and that bumpiness and loss of speed are still apparent. The fastest track in England – Welwyn – is one smooth surface of bitumen, with no seams).

Thus Welwyn and Nottingham are now putting the cement tracks such as Manchester, Cardiff and Paddington out of date. Cardiff and Paddington must be rated as the two fastest cement surfaces in the country; both however, being slower than Welwyn and Nottingham.

In 1892 also, the N.C.U. decided to 'licence' riders, for the first time. A *Cycling* editorial of the time commented: 'Why not keep 'em in kennels, and feed 'em on Spratt's too?' (*Cycling's* editor at the time was Poly man Walter Groves).

In those days, all the big clubs were 'based' on one particular track, which they regarded as 'home ground', and they were more or less responsible for the continuity of a season-long racing programme on that track. Thus we find the following 'pairings' in those days – London County club on the London County Grounds, Herne Hill; Polytechnic C.C. on Paddington; Manchester A.C. on Fallowfield; Catford club on Catford track; Wood Green C. & A.C. on Wood Green track; Putney B.C. on Putney Velodrome; North Road C.C. on St Albans track; and so on.

(Most of the famous tracks of the 'nineties, including Putney, Wood Green, Crystal Palace, Canning Town, Kensal Rise, St Albans, Catford, Olympia, Celtic Park, etc., have vanished under the tide of bricks and mortar; but Herne Hill, Paddington, and Fallowfield remain as reminders of the glory that was cycling).

In later years, the London County club passed away, although a plaque in the grandstand at Herne Hill still recalls their memory; and the Poly 'moved in' at Herne Hill; the Marlboro A.C. 'taking over' at Paddington. But in 1892, when the Marlboro was formed, it was a Cricket and Athletics Club, the cycling interest coming in and predominating at the turn of the century.

Nowadays, the Track Leagues perform this 'continuity of promotion' business; the vast number of small non-promoting clubs have sapped the potential strength of the older and more stable organizations, by way of cheap subscriptions and easily-gained membership. (The older and more knowledgeable clubs still continue to supply the bulk of promoting and organising officials to the Ruling Bodies, however).

In 1892, Paddington track was described by such authorities as G Lacy Hillier and Dr E B Turner (the famous one-eyed record-breaker, N.C.U. Judge, England International footballer, and Poly C.C. vice-president), as 'the finest racing path in the country'. Commenting on the records put up by W C Jones, Poly, from ½ to 5 miles, the *Graphic* newspaper of 20th September, 1890, refers to 'the fast Paddington track'.

The Paddington track was built in 1888, at a cost of £5,000; the surface being composed of 'cinders, brickdust, burnt clay, and coal-dust' according to Lacy Hillier. Spectator accommodation in 1892 at Paddington, consisted of a grandstand at the home-straight, plus a long covered enclosure at the backstraight. The enclosure was constructed of thin posts and wire-netting, with a floor of rubble.

Inevitably it became known as the 'Chicken Run', and the denizens of the Chicken Run were noted for their witty (and otherwise) comments on the racing. They were extremely vociferous, whenever 'waiting tactics', known then as 'loafing' took place; but the 'go-all-the-way' style of riders, such as 'Jennie' Walters, Jack Still, Ernie Leitch, Bert Harris, and Jack Camp (all Polymen), were their idols. Jack Still, in fact (like Harris, a 'Humber' rider), was referred to in the December, 1892, *Poly C.C. Gazette* as 'the favourite of the Paddington Chicken Run'.

Bert's Paddington debut was in May, '92, as a member of the Polytechnic team in a match against the London County Club. Alf Edwards, tall good-looking N.C.U. London Champion, captained the Poly team. (Bert stayed with Alf's family on his first London trip, and also on subsequent visits; and paid great tribute to the individual coaching he received from Alf in 1892). The London County team was captained by A A Zimmerman, a 'Raleigh' rider, American crack sprinter, and future World Champion. ('Zimmy' was World Sprint Champion of '93).

Many fables have grown up around the riders of the 'nineties, and the one about 'Zimmy' and his low gear (always 5 to 8 inches less than his rivals), is well-known. What isn't so well known is the fact that he used cranks only 6 inches in length, which of course puts the story in a different light.

Nevertheless, Zimmerman was outstanding as a stylist, even in a period when style was a 'sine qua non' for every racing cyclist. In the Sprint race of this match, Bert lost by inches only, after a thrilling duel with Zimmerman, his rival in many professional races in later years. Zimmy was born at Camden, New Jersey, in 1869; and died in 1936, aged 67.

(Actually, Bert was suffering from a heavy cold, and the June, '92, *Poly C.C. Gazette*' describes him as 'not being at all well' at the meeting. He had picked up a cold at the Easter Tuesday meet at Manchester, held on a very cold day, when Alf Edwards, Bert Harris, and A T Mole, all Poly, had taken 1st, 2nd and 3rd in the Sprint race. Poly Midland Section rider Teddy Young suffered a crash at this meeting, and had a pedal wound behind his ear).

'Taffy' Davies, the legendary Polytechnic old-timer, in waggish mood, told the author that, 'Harris wore as his out-door costume, a Cinnamon Brown suit; the prevailing fashion of the time. This probably accounted for his defeat by Zimmerman!' At that time (1892), 'Taffy' was a lordly 20 years old, compared with Bert's 18! Polytechnic nevertheless won the Match, bringing joy to the hearts of the Kilburn bookies, as the punters had backed Zimmy's team confidently, trusting in the 'American Express' to inspire the County team. Alf Edwards and Ernie Leitch also distinguished themselves on this occasion; the weather was perfect, 'the Poly flag hanging limply from its mast' betokening ideal racing conditions. (Vide *Poly C.C. Gazette*).

At Whitsun, Bert collected a 1st and a 2nd, and the friendship ripened between the 5ft. 2in. Bert and the 6ft. 1in. Alf Edwards. They had much in common; both rode the 'Humber' machine, both were skilled billiards players, didn't take girls seriously, and were a pair of pranksters, notorious for their practical jokes and tomfoolery. On one occasion they broke away in a '5', stayed away for 9 laps, linked arms for the last $\frac{1}{2}$ lap, and bowled up the home-straight whistling 'Daisy, Daisy', the Bicycle Belle song. Zimmerman, in winning the N.C.U. National 1-mile and 5-mile titles in July, 1892, gave the two pals something else in common – two 2nd-place medals; Alf being 2nd in the Mile, and Bert 2nd in the 'Five'. These events were run off on Headingley grasstrack, near Leeds. Headingley is now a famous cricket ground.

(In those days, and in fact right up to 1935, when the German Toni Merkens won the Sprint tilte, the N.C.U. National Championships were open to the World).

Bert, together with Percy Brown, a Poly sprinter of note, were invited to race in America in 1892, but declined as it would have meant missing the National Championships mentioned above.

Bert Harris, 5ft. 2in. of cycling fury, and Alf Edwards, his own especial clubmate, tall, languid-looking, and unruffled in the roughest racing, took the fancy of promoters, who gave them star billing; the crowds took 'little 'Arris' to their hearts. Alf won the

Poly club track championship in 1892. In those days, the Track Championship was held over 5 miles only, instead of the two events – Sprint and Five – that are run off these days.

In May, '92, the Manchester A.C. had opened what they described as 'the fastest shale track in England'. (And so in fact it was; and remained so until 1950, when Reg Harris bought it and resurfaced it with pink cement). This new track cost £4,000 to build, and was named 'Fallowfield'. On July 16th, at the Salford Harriers meet, Bert made his Fallowfield debut, winning the sprint event. The following week was the Manchester A.C's Charity Tournament, July 23rd, on the same track.

Bert won the 880 Sprint, beating Osmond. Ernie Leitch, Bert's Poly clubmate, won the 'Five', with Bert 2nd, after the two Poly boys had broken away to a ½-lap lead which they held to the finish.

Bespectacled Ernie had previously made a great impression at Herne Hill in early July, by soundly trouncing the great Zimmerman in a sprint event. Leitch at this time lived in Nottingham, where he was an executive of the 'Humber' Cycle Company at Beeston. He got Harris to ride the 'Humber', and Bert, after 1892, never used any other make of 'jigger' throughout his career, both as Amateur and Professional.

'Humber' were the first to build a true Diamond frame, in 1891; ruthlessly scrapping the short chainstays and curved seat-tube of the period, and replacing them with chainstays long enough to permit the use of a straight seat-tube. (Curiously enough, the curved seat-tube is now coming back into fashion!).

The Poly Club had an invite in 1892 to Dublin, for a return match against du Cros and his boys, who wanted revenge for their 1891 defeat at Paddington. Bert, Alf and Ernie were of course included in the Team, and a group photograph taken at the time shows a very youthful-looking Bert, with his Poly buttonhole badge (twice the size of the modern Poly badge) quite evident, and a fashionable gold watch-chain draped across his fancy waistcoat.

Bert was always very proud of his Poly membership; and once, when twitted about joining a Club with its H.Q. 100 miles away from his home, he replied simply, 'I'll always be first-claim Poly'.

As the knowledgable cyclist knows, the Midland Section of the Poly, started in 1889 is actually the oldest-established Cycling Group in Leicestershire; the Leics. R.C. being the next oldest, formed in 1908. The Midland Section of Bert's time included such famous racers as Herbert Synyer, Ernie Leitch, C W Schafer, Teddy Young, W Griffiths, Sam Bailey and Harris himself. Even in modern times, many National and International honours have been won by Poly Midland Section riders; the names of Archer, Brotherton, McCarthy, Tong and Whitfield, spring to mind, for the 1950's to 1960's period.

The match versus the Irish Champion club was at Dublin on 10th August, 1892. The Poly were beaten by the narrow margin of 2 points; the visitors being 'none too happy with the awkward corners of the Balls Bridge track', as Walter Groves put it. 'The boys were treated right royally at Dublin and Waterford, where special meetings were held', commented Groves, who besides being Editor of *Cycling* was also Editor of the *Poly C.C. Gazette*. The August issue of the latter periodical made great play with Bert's victory over the famous Johnny Adams at Long Eaton in July, '92. On September 17th, Bert ended the season with a visit to Herne Hill, breaking the National 1-mile Record with a time of 2 mins. 8 and 1/5th secs. On Thursday, 15th December, 1892, Bert, together with Walter Groves, Jack Still, Ernie Leitch, Teddy Day, and other 'Polyites', helped Alf Edwards to celebrate his 21st birthday.

According to Groves, Bert's tongue was loosened under the influence of 'a few', and he gave quite a vigorous and memorable performance. On the way home, Bert also 'displayed great calisthenic talent in the wee small hours of the morning'. Also in December Bert, Alf and Ernie were presented with 'massive silver Polytechnic Institute medals' for their notable 1892 performances. The magazine *Cycling* instituted a postal vote among its readers at the end of November, to elect the 'Twelve Trackmen of the Year'. The result was displayed on an Illustrated Art Folder presented with *Cycling* in December. Zimmerman was 1st, Bert

Harris 2nd, and Alf Edwards 3rd. Ernie Leitch was also one of the five(!) Poly men pictured in this elite dozen.

Annoyed Midlanders, jealous of Bert's membership of a London club, referred to him as the 'Poly Provincial Pup'. Characteristically, Bert was highly delighted and amused at this and had 'P.P.P.' stencilled on his travelling bag.

(Modern Midlanders are more tolerant, and the Poly's Midland Section, with its H.Q. in Leicester, is held in high regard by the 'locals').

Bert actually won more First Prizes than any other rider in England in the 1892 Season; according to the *Poly C.C. Gazette* of January, 1893, his total Opens Prize Value for the year amounted to over £600.

An American newspaper correspondent, 'Whirligig', had the last word on the Harris 1892 Season, with the soubriquet, 'Modest little Harris'.

Ernie Leitch, Midland Section secretary of the Poly, was married in December, 1892, which meant another party for Bert.

CHAPTER FIVE

FAMILY TROUBLES

IN JANUARY, 1893, BERT'S MOTHER DIED in one of Leicester's regular epidemics, at the early age of 41. Leicester in Victorian and Edwardian days, was just about the most unhygienic city in England, and was the despair of successive Health Officers of the town, who came and went in quick succession; resigning after futile battles against 'ignorance in High Places'. (Vide Local Histories and Newspapers of the time).

Bert was grief-stricken and inconsolable for some weeks; he'd been extremely 'close' to his Mother, who 'worried herself skinny' during his racing absences from home.

A photo' in *The Wheeler* of February, 1893, shows Bert, who definitely does not wear his customary merry look, held up by his Father; the latter wearing a black armband.

Bert is depicted on his 'Humber', with 2 inch Dunlops on wired-on rims; 30 inch front wheel, 28 inch rear; Brooks B.19 saddle; 'Perry' block chain; and a typical wide, deep handle-bar bend. His 'bars are however, rather more forward than his contemporaries, and he has quite a daring (for the time) forward tilt to his body.

In February, '93, Leitch moved down to Hampstead (N.W. London) and Edwards took up a job as manager of a cycle depot in Newcastle.

Bert's old schoolmate Will Jordan, together with Joe Aram of Beeston, contrived to occupy his mind with a new interest – tandem riding. Bert 'palled up' with Aram, and they raced at Liverpool over Easter, 1893, Bert collecting a 2nd and 3rd, and

Aram a Lap Prize. Bert's next win was the 'Brookes Cup' at the 'Sport and Play' tournament at Aston track, Birmingham – for the 3rd year in succession, so this 25 guinea trophy was now his for keeps.

Herne Hill at this time sported a fast wooden surface, made of 2 inch battens; it was however very dangerous when wet. Kensal Rise had fallen from favour, and Paddington had a new, cement surface. Bert's bag for April, '93, was 7 firsts and 1 second. In May he collected 11 firsts and 1 second. In June, 4 firsts, 3 seconds, 2 thirds.

June was a busy month for Harris; he raced to 2nd place in the N.C.U. National 1 mile Championship 'on the wood' at Herne Hill, being beaten by Walter Sanger (U.S.A.); then got 2nd in the National 'Five', being beaten by clubmate Alec Watson.

Incidentally, the late F T Bidlake, the North Road C.C. historian, attributed Bert's defeat in the 'Mile' to his use of the heavy wired-on Dunlop tyres and rims. Sanger was using Palmer 'single-tubes' as they were called by their American makers. In England, such tyres were known as 'tube-tyres' (vide Lacy Hillier, etc.), at this time. The first tyres of this type, the English 'Boothroyd' had been merely a tube encased in a canvas tubular jacket. There was no means of withdrawing the tube for repair, and the method of mending a puncture was by the insertion of small rubber plugs into the perforation. The chafing of the canvas also brought constant trouble to 'Boothroyd' users.

Then 'Palmer' tube-tyres appeared in America, with the casing made of a specially-designed anti-chafe material – two layers of diagonal threaded material, laid alternately in 'X' fashion. They were still not made with a removable inner tube, and punctures were still repaired with tiny rubber plugs. The new slim, smooth treaded, all-black Palmers were very fast and lively, and were immediately dubbed 'hosepipes' by English trackmen.

It wasn't long before all the 'heads' were using them; Bert himself rode them in the latter half of the 1893 Season, and kept to them, in conjunction with 'Jointless' hollow rims, for his Professional career.

(In 1895, the Palmer tyre was manufactured under licence in

FAMILY TROUBLES

England, and was without doubt the most successful racing tyre in the World up till the turn of the century).

Tubular tyres are still known to this day, in America and Australia, as 'singles'. The French tyre concern, Michelin, brought out a tubular tyre in red rubber known as 'Le Paris', which was used by Linton and Michael in 1894. 'Le Paris' was sold at 7/6d. each, by the British agents for the 'Gladiator' (French) cycle, who had a showroom in Holborn, London. Later still, in 1895, the Italian 'Pirelli' tubulars were imported by A W Gamage – (yes, the famous Department Store). Gamage was a keen cyclist and Poly C.C. member.

When the British riders started using 'Palmers', Sanger was soon cut down to size'. The first two British riders to beat him were Poly men Percy Brown and Tommy Gibbons-Brooks. W Glynn, another Poly C.C. man, took up Palmer's English agency, and was the proprietor of the concern already mentioned, making 'Palmers' under licence in this country, with an office in London and branches in Coventry and Birmingham. Later still, Poly man Studor Brown, a noted N.C.U. handicapper of the 'nineties, brought out a rival racing tyre, the 'Seddon'. This, like the 'Michelin', was red, and was known among the boys as the 'Red 'Un'. 'Red 'uns' were used by such noted riders as Alec Watson, Tommy Osborn, Percy Brown, G L Morris (all Poly), and Scheltema-Beduin (Catford). (Studor Brown went insane in 1898, and was confined in Colney Hatch asylum).

Annoyed with himself for his two 2nd place medals in the National Championships, Bert attacked the National 5 miles Record on June 10th, at Herne Hill, and broke it. By now, he was getting over his Mother's death, and was more like his old cheerful self. A trip to the Isle of Man netted him 3 'firsts' at Douglas.

Bert collected 8 'firsts' in July, including Trophy wins at Torquay and Plymouth. In the West Country Bert took a liking to Devon cream, and was 'twitted' about his fondness for cream, in the Club Magazine.

Next came an International Match, 'England v. Scotland'; the English team composed of three Poly men – Alec Watson, Bert

Harris, and Percy Brown. The English (Poly) team won easily. On the return journey they called in at Newcastle, where Alf Edwards (now a 2nd claim member of the Newcastle club), was promoting the Newcastle Centre 5 mile Championship. (In those days, Centre titles were open to all comers).

The three Poly boys, Watson, Brown and Harris, took 1st, 2nd and 3rd respectively, from a field of 31 riders. The meeting was run off on the North Durham track, Newcastle. In August, Bert took 9 'firsts', including the 'Coventry Cup' for the 3rd year running. Then back to London for the *Cycling Cup*, on Paddington track. The Final was an all-Poly affair, with Alec Watson 1st, Percy Brown 2nd, Bert Harris 3rd, and Jack Camp 4th.

(It's noticeable that the few riders who ever beat Bert were either Poly men, or World-class foreigners).

A visit to Denmark in late August and early September netted Bert 5 more prizes.

Then came the Polytechnic Club Championship, in September on Paddington track.

Cycling forecast an 'interesting race' – it was!

The field included all the National-class Poly men, such as Brown, Watson, Harris, Edwards, Leitch, Tommy Osborn, Jack Still, Alf Mole, Gibbons-Brooks, Jack Camp, etc. – all top-class riders and prolific prizewinners. Bert won, after a young newcomer, A E Walters, had repeatedly stirred up the pace and split the field to shreds. Bert was very proud of his Club Championship victory; it was sweet solace for his defeat by Watson in the National 'Five' and he declared himself 'immensely pleased'. Ernie Leitch made it a 'double' for the Midlands, by winning the 1893 Club 100 mile Road Championship.

It was to be another 69 years before another Leicester rider took a Poly Club title; Roger Whitfield winning the Junior Sprint trophy, the 'Enfield Cup'; in 1962 at Welwyn track.

Bert's racing 'Humber', with a fiercer-than-ever handlebar, was enamelled Royal Blue; it weighed $22\frac{1}{2}$ lbs.; rather heavy by comparison with the 18 lbs of the 'Demon' and the 19 lbs. of the 'Nelson', other typical trackirons of 1893. The 'Demon' was

Aston Track, Easter 1897. Bert Harris winning the 440 yards Sprint, with Carl Smitz second. Later, in the 10 Miles, Harris was fatally injured.

Bert Harris after winning the National Amateur Championship in 1891 ('Humber' bicycle) (Photo courtesy of Cycling*)*

*Bert Harris, Club Track Champion of the Polytechnic C.C. 1893
(held by his father)
(Photo: The Wheeler)*

The Harris Trophy

Bert Harris was National Amateur Champion of 1891 and National Professional Champion of 1894. The Trophy is awarded to the winner of the 5 Mile Championship of the Midlands Section of the Polytechnic Cycling Club.

The twelve best path racers of 1891 as chosen by the vote of Cycling's readers. (reproduced from Cycling, *October 24, 1891)*

FAMILY TROUBLES

made by Poly rider Paine, in Crawford Street, Marylebone, London.

The 'Nelson' was marketed by another Poly man, A W Gamage, whose cycle depot grew into the mammoth Gamage's Department Store in later years. Other notable Poly cycle traders of the time were ex-Club Captain George L Morris, M.C.E.I., who manufactured the beautiful 'Referee' racing bikes, with the patent 'triple head' at his works in 66, Turnmill Street, Farringdon Road, London, E.C.

Morris, Poly Captain from 1885-8, had been 3rd in the National 1-mile Championship of 1889. Another well-known Poly cycle-shop was run by the Panzetta Brothers, who specialised in 'Triumph' racers at their Depot at 287, Upper Street, Islington, North London. Panzetta's branch shop at 72, Charing Cross Road, was managed by Poly boy Frank Rhodes. Taffy Davies was manager of the Jarvis Cycle Co., owned by Poly C.C. man Ted Jarvis. W A Vincent was manager of the Puncture-Proof Tyre Co.; Teddy Young was manager of the Campion Cycle Co., owned by Poly man Harry Campion (the 'Campion 12-hours Shield' was donated by Harry in 1893); Studor Brown was 'Raglan' manager; W T Walton was at 'Swift's'; Charles Friswell owned a Cycle shop at 207A, Pentonville Road, London, N.; and J Rickard was a lightweight maker. I Tourunnen, Poly C.C. and 1894 National Champion of Finland, marketed the patent 'Invincible' cycle-stand at 1, Leadenhall Street, E.C. London. (Tourunnen died in Finland in August, 1899. He won 3 National Championships of Finland in his racing career, and was a First-Claim Poly man all his cycling life).

With Leitch at 'Humbers', Schafer ('Peregrine'), and Alf Edwards, manager of a cycle shop, the Trade influence was strong in the club.

Poly boy J. Mason, manager for Gamage 1891-2, moved to the 'New Howe' firm in July, 1893, as general manager. His place at Gamage's was taken by Gibbons-Brooks. Bobby Burns, after losing his job after his crash in the National '25' of June, 1892, got a job as Traveller for the 'New Howe' firm. All the people named above, were active Poly racing men.

In 1893, 30 inch front wheels were still standard for racers, with 28 inch rear; in 1894 began the gradual change-over to equal-sized wheels of 28 in. diameter. Bert stayed on in London after the Club Championship, and in a great attack on National Records at Herne Hill, collected the following:

September 14 ½ mile (61 3/5 secs.). Mile (2m. 7 2/5 secs.).
September 21 Tandem ¼ mile (26 4/5) tandem Mile (2m. 2 4/5) (With J Aram as tandem partner).
September 22 440 yds. in 27 1/5 secs.
October 3 Mile in 2m. 4 1/5 secs.
October 12 2 miles; 4 mins. 20 secs.

In November, 1893, his portrait was included in 'Cassell's Illustrated Almanac' as 'Cyclist of the Year'.

At the Club Dinner on November 4th at the Holborn Restaurant, it was noted that 'Bert Harris, on receiving his Club Championship award, did not speechify; his modesty once more standing him in good stead', (vide *Poly C.C. Gazette*).

As an Amateur, Bert had certainly tried hard to live up to *Cycling's* tag of 'the invincible Bert Harris'. He had beaten the best men of his time – Adams, Osmond, Good, Fowler, Zimmerman, Thistleton, Pope, Scheltema-Beduin, Fentiman, Bradbury; and all the great Poly 'men of class', including Watson, Brown, Leitch, Lambley, Gibbons-Brooks, etc. He was never out of the first two in any National Championship he entered, and this was a habit he carried forward into his Professional career.

Bert was always a 'man's man', treating womenfolk with exaggerated courtesy, always mourning secretly for his Mother, and making friends slowly.

Every friend he made, however, admired and respected Harris unreservedly; and this is quite evident from comments by contemporaries. He was a champion rider at the height of the Cycle-racing craze, and rode the crest of a wave of popularity and adulation. Bert's old rival and Poly clubmate, Alec Watson, reminiscing in 1962 when he was over 90 years old, said, 'Harris, Edwards, and myself were on the National Scratch Mark, in handicaps. We had some great races. I well recall the racing trips with the Poly teams to Ireland, Denmark and France. Great times they were'.

G H Knight, captain of the Newhaven club in the 'nineties, and a regular visitor to London tracks, referred to Bert Harris as 'a very fine personality'.

CHAPTER SIX

PROFESSIONAL!

IN 1894 BERT HARRIS, ALF EDWARDS, and Alf's tandem partner Green (Newcastle), all turned professional. Bert signed for 'Humber' and Alf for 'Rudge'; the Press spoke of 'these lucrative engagements'.

Bert and Alf, after buying their travelling trunks from a Polytechnic man, Warner, who was in that line of business, left England in January, 1894, and set up a bachelor establishment in the Boulevard Delessert, Paris, near the Seine, within a mile of the Paris indoor track. They set to work to 'polish up' for their new careers. Bert and Alf certainly 'polished up' in no mean fashion, winning prizes and prestige on the indoor velodrome. Then a trip to Italy, where Bert won a Sprint Match against French and Italian riders; Edwards and Green on the tandem shattered all opposition in tandem-racing. (When Edwards and Green came back to England for the National Professional Championship, they were matched against a trio of crack Americans – Johnson, Weinig and Peters – on a triplet. Edwards and Green won easily).

Returning home for the Professional Championship of England, held in Birmingham on the Aston Lower Grounds track, the pair of Poly lads proved their Continetal form wasn't a flash-in-the-pan, by taking 1st (Bert) and 2nd (Alf) places in the Championship, held over 1 mile (4 laps). An invite to Leicester followed, and on the Aylestone Road track Zimmerman and Harris finished half-a-lap ahead of the field, in a 5 miles (15 laps) race. (Zimmerman had signed pro. forms for the 'Raleigh' concern, at the end of 1893).

About this time, Bert was approached by a Music-Hall Agent, who wanted to write a sketch around him and put him 'on the Halls'. Harris declined, and later referred to it with vast amusement, in a conversation with Alf Edwards and Tommy Osborn. ('Going on the Halls' was a common fate of most outstanding sportsmen of the 'nineties, as witness the boxers, jockeys and rifle-shots who were so treated in those days).

The two pals made a point of witnessing the Polytechnic Club Track Championship of 1894, both being ex-holders of the title, Alf in 1892 and Bert in 1893.

The 1894 event fell to Tommy Osborn, with Percy Brown 2nd and Jack Camp 3rd. Both Osborn and Brown rode the triple-head 'Referee' machines made by Morris (Poly). This was in early September. (Percy Brown had previously taken 3rd place in the World's 1-mile Championship at Antwerp, in August. This indicates the quality of Tommy Osborn!).

After this the two young professionals, with the added lustre of being the two top men in their country at their profession, returned to Paris – where they acted as guides for a party of Poly boys who'd come over for an end-of-season tour. 1894 was a happy year for Bert, especially as his boy-hood ambition of following his old hero, Bob English, as National Professional Champion, had been fulfilled.

One of Bert's Midlands Section pals, Sam Bailey, moved South at this time (September, 1894), and became 'mine host' of the 'Black Boy' public house, on the main road between Henley and Maidenhead.

A whole page of the *Poly C.C. Gazette* was taken up in the September issue, with a story of Perce Brown's defeat in the 'World's' (mentioned above). The Antwerp track was a freak, with a narrow flat part on the inside, permitting of only 2 riders abreast. The remaining width was made up of a 45-degree banking. Curiously enough, when the World's Pro-Sprint Championship of 1920 was held at Antwerp on the same track, another Poly boy, Bill Bailey (who had previously won four Amateur

Sprint Championships of the World), made the same mistake as Brown, by 'laying off' in third position in the Final. In 1894 National colours weren't 'de rigeur', and the three Poly men who represented England, namely Osborn, Brown and Watson, raced in their Poly vests. They also wore white caps with the Rose of England embroidered upon the fronts. The Rose badge continued as a National emblem for many years, and even in the 1930's the winner of English National Championships was awarded a Rose Badge for sewing on to his racing vest.

CHAPTER SEVEN

DISASTER

1895 DAWNED AS A GOLDEN OPPORTUNITY for Bert, as reigning National Professional Champion. His first engagement was an Easter invitation to Cardiff track for a match against Welsh Pro. Champion Tom James, for £50 and the title 'Champion of England and Wales'. Bert won the first race of the match; but in the second race he was deliberately fouled by James, who 'bored him into the rails', to quote *The Hub* reporter. 'He was fouled in the most barefaced manner by James, and has sustained serious injuries', said the *Poly C.C. Gazette* of April, 1895. 'Harris would undoubtedly have won the match had it not been for the foul riding of James, who was disqualified by the Referee'.

(The Referee approximated to our modern 'B.C.F. Observer' at trackmeets in those days, but had power to over-rule the Judge).

'We have no doubt the Union will have something to say respecting James's riding. This is clearly a case where the Union should stop a man from racing at all', continues the angry *Poly C.C. Gazette* reporter. The N.C.U. did have something to say and James had his Licence withdrawn, was 'warned off' all tracks, and suspended for life, by the N.C.U. for this affair.

Bert, of course, won the match by default.

Harris's injuries included a split eardrum, and he never fully recovered from the effects of this crash. His hearing and sense of balance was affected; he suffered from occasional giddy spells, and even his memory was affected.

After a stay in Cardiff Hospital, Bert was taken by his Father to Droitwich Spa for recuperative treatment. The hot salt baths of the 'Royal Brine Baths' establishment did Bert 'a power of good' and in June he started training for a come-back.

The *Poly C.C. Gazette* for June, '95, said: 'All Poly boys will rejoice that the Professional Champion of England is fast recovering from the effects of his nasty spill at Cardiff. It is marvellous how soon he has got better, considering the seriousness of the smash. He still occasionally feels dizzy, but this we hope will soon wear off. Bert wishes to be kindly remembered to you all'.

Bert did, indeed make a determined effort to get fit, and on June 22nd at Herne Hill he gained 2nd in the National Professional Mile Championship of 1895; Protin (Belgium) was 1st, and Charley Barden 3rd. (The National 5 mile Amateur title was won in the same meeting by A J Watson, Poly).

Protin went on to win the Professional Sprint Championship of the World in Germany the following month. Barden went on to win the N.C.U. National Professional Championship in 1896, with his rival of the old Kensal Rise days Tommy Osborn (Poly) in 2nd place; and Alf Edward's tandem partner Green in 3rd position. (Barden was 2nd in the World Pro. Sprint Championship of 1896 and again in 1897).

At this time, the height of the Professional Cycling business in this country, there were dozens of pro. riders, and hundreds of paid pacers, with tandems, triplets, quads, and quints. Cycle-racing was Big Business.

(Nowadays our pro. class is about a dozen all told – so Poly boys Ricketts, Burgess and Brotherton represent 25 per cent of England's professional strength!).

During his stay in hospital Bert had grown a moustache, and this occasioned much leg-pulling by the Poly boys.

Back to France again, to the hurly-burly of the tough, fast Paris 'school'. After the National Mile, the *Poly C.C. Gazette* had commented: 'Harris's riding in the Professional Championship was splendid. He is rapidly recovering his old dash'. This wasn't just wishful thinking; Bert really was full of 'zip', and his victims in Paris included Australian 'flier' Joe Megson, trade rival Alf Edwards, and Frenchman Bourillon, who was to become World Pro. Sprint Champion in 1896. In 1898 Bourillon retired from racing to become an Opera Singer. In late July, 1895, the 'Humber' Cycle Works was burnt down. In August, Bert visited the temporary Works where the Works Manager, Walter Phillips, made quite a fuss of Bert. Phillips had taken the Professional 100 miles Championship at Leicester in 1879, and knew the Harris family well, having raced in Leicester up till 1883. Phillips suggested a Record Attempt on the super-fast Catford cement track, which was as sensational in its day as the super-fast Welwyn is in the nineteen-sixties. Bert took the Professional Half-Mile and Professional Mile, National Records, with the times of 57, 2/5th secs. and 1 min. 58, 2/5 secs., respectively. This was in early September. His last engagement for '95 was a pro. match on Aston track, where his Paris rival, Australian Joe Megson, took 1st, with Bert 3rd. Megson, together with R Lewis and E Payne, was to meet Bert again . . . this time in their own country, after their successful European visit. Giant photographs of Bert, with replicas of his machine, were displayed in the Holborn Viaduct showrooms of 'Humber'; for in those days, the Viaduct was the Cycle Trade Headquarters of London, with Rudge, Referee, Raleigh, Humber, Centaur, Rover, etc., competing for attention with displays of trophies, racing irons, Championship sashes, giant photographs, polished floors, and smartly-dressed salesmen.

'Humber's' showroom was at 32, Holborn Viaduct; 'Raleigh's' were at No. 41, 'Swift's' were at No. 15. Other Holborn showrooms included 'Rudge', 'Crypto', 'Dunlop', 'Triumph', 'Juno', 'Gamage', and dozens of others.

Alf Edwards was still in Italy, fulfilling racing engagements for August and September. Bert went home to Leicester for an easy 'off spell', and marvelled at the way Leicester was changing. His father, and old friends Will Jordan and Joe Aram, gave Bert a grand time, but he worried his father with his frequent visits to his mother's grave; Harris senior referred to it as 'unhealthy' in a conversation with Jordan.

At this time, Leicester was expanding rapidly; new houses were being built in every direction; there was talk of steam trams replacing the old horse-drawn trams along the Belgrave route; but most of Leicester's streets were still stone setts, very uncomfortable for cycling. (Many are unchanged to this day; thus giving the 'lie direct' to local boasts of being a 'prosperous city').

CHAPTER EIGHT

'HARRIS YEAR'

MEANTIME, ON THE OTHER SIDE OF THE WORLD, Alex Leith (who'd been Poly C.C. secretary in 1886), was working on a scheme for a Harris racing visit to Australia. Leith, who'd been Poly C.C. treasurer 1887-1893, was a Vice-President of the Club, and had emigrated to Australia in 1894. 1896 was to be Bert's best-ever season, and Australian newspapers referred to it, in retrospect, as 'Harris-Year'. He rode in Melbourne, Bendigo, Warnambool, Portland, Kilmore, Ballarat and Hamilton – even on one occasion making the 400 miles trip to Sydney, to race on the brand new cement track there. He beat his old rival Megson at Sydney; Megson, paced by a 'quint', knocked out a 'Flying Quarter' of 21, 3/5th secs. the following week on the same track!

(The Sydney track was broken up in 1920. From 1882 to 1895 regular grasstrack meets were held there, and H L Cortis, the old English High Bicycle champion, was an official at some of these meets, having emigrated to Australia).

Incidentally, the 'Sydney Trophy', raced for at the old Oval meets and promoted by the Surrey B.C. – and which Bert had won three times – was actually presented to the Surrey club by this Sydney club of Australia. When the Sydney club had first been formed, the English club had given the new club a trophy to help get them started; the 'Sydney Trophy' was a reciprocal gift. Bert's Australian trip was an unqualified success. At one period he won 15 first prizes in succession, on clay, cinder, grass and cement-surfaced tracks. Melbourne, as befitted the capital of

Victoria State, had a modern cement track, and provided the high spot of the tour. This was a match against the Australian Professional Champion, Parsons, for a £400 first prize.

Harris won it; causing much mental anguish and pecuniary loss to the Australian 'bookies'. (Betting was probably the most important aspect of Australian bike-racing). Bert's total 'bag' in Australia was over £800 in cash, plus a collection of trophies totalling nearly £300. (Work that out in modern currency values!).

Curiously enough, although Zimmerman was also racing in Australia in 1896, the old rivals didn't meet in competition in Aussie. Zimmerman's professional career, curiously enough, had not come up to the promise of his wonderful Amateur performances.

The Australian Summer, and therefore Track season, falls during our Winter, so while Bert was 'hammering the natives' in Aussie, at home in England his Poly clubmates, A E Walters, A J Watson, T Osborn, T Gibbons-Brooks and E Winbolt, were signing Professional Contracts for the 1896 season. (Winbolt died in the Klondyke Gold rush, spring of 1898).

Bert's visit to Australia co-incided with a great Bicycling Craze in that Continent. Lord Brassey, the Governor of Victoria State (according to the July, 1897, issue of *Lady's Realm*), had to sell his tricycle and buy a two-wheeler in order to keep up with his wife and daughter on their cycle-rides around Melbourne. Lady Brassey, in fact, was so 'potty' about Cycling, that she put on a 'Musical Bicycle-Ride' in the ballroom of Government House, Melbourne – then reputed to be the largest ballroom in the World – as the 'piece-de-resistance' of the first Vice-Regal Ball of 1896. Naturally, the Society Sheep followed suit dutifully and so the colonial belles, known locally as 'cyclodonnas', flocked to buy bicycles. 'Humbers' did very well in the ensuing boom, tying up their adverts with Bert's racing victories.

A picture in the same issue of the above-mentioned *Lady's Realm*', shows a great banner dominating the arena of the Velodrome de la Madelaine in Paris, advertising 'Cycles Whitworth'.

'HARRIS YEAR'

Add to this the enormous demand for 'Raleigh' cycles in America (Raleighs, of course, had 'Zimmy' racing for them), and it's easy to understand that the British Cycle of the nineties occupied the same honoured position that the Italian Cycle does in the 1960's – that is, leaders in both Design and Workmanship. (In fact, the highest praise that can be given to a British Bicycle these days, is that it is of 'Italian Design!').

On leaving Australia in May, '96, Bert was presented with a Testimonial (plus cash) by 'The Sportsmen of Victoria – who, one suspects, were composed mainly of satisfied betting men! England, however, had been 'enjoying' a typical traditional wet English Spring and this was followed by a cold wet Summer. It took Bert some little time to re-acclimatise himself and settle down to some serious training.

He went along to Herne Hill to see his old rival Percy Brown (Poly) win the N.C.U. Amateur Mile Championship of England, with W Bardsley (Poly) 2nd, and 'Acky' Ingram (Poly) 3rd. The Press made great play with this all-Poly final. Bardsley (Poly) followed up by winning the National 50 miles Championship, in 1 hr. 57 mins. 28 4/5 secs.

Percy had joined the Poly at the same time as Bert; he lived about 100 yards away from the Poly Institute, and 'put Bert up' for the night on this occasion. Another clubman and rival, Alec Watson, was now a pro. – and 'Jennie' Walters, on a 'Humber' (with a Simpson lever chain), was thus a pro. stablemate of Bert's. Bert 'got down to it' in July, and did a little racing in August, experimenting with a 92 inch gear in place of his customary 84.

He also corresponded with many friends he'd made in Australia, and in an interview with *The Hub* reporter professed himself 'delighted' with his reception in the Antipodes. 'It is a grand place for sport', he said, 'The people there go mad on cycle-racing'. He loved 'Aussie' and stated his intention of settling 'Down Under' as soon as the 1897 Season was over. Alas – poor Bert never finished the 1897 Season.

At this time, Ernie Leitch was on the way to Australia, emigrating there with a job in a cycle firm in Sydney.

(This may have influenced Bert's decision to emigrate, and it's quite possible the two Midlanders had some business deal in mind – such as opening a Cycle Shop. But this of course, is only surmise).

CHAPTER NINE

PREMONITION

FROM NOW ON, the Harris story becomes a fantastic tangle of coincidence and controversy.

On Easter Saturday, 1897, Bert was due to race at Bolton. He was restless and depressed, and when the train reached Derby he was in such a state of nervous tension that his father persuaded him to turn back to Leicester. Bert told his father that he had a sense of impending doom. That night he couldn't sleep; went downstrairs and sat up with his father for a while; and at length went to bed for a fitful sleep. On the Sunday morning he took his bike and pottered off through the lanes towards Melton Mowbray, but couldn't shake off the terrible feeling of dread.

On the Monday he was booked to race at the inaugural meet on the newly-rebuilt $\frac{1}{4}$ mile steeply-banked cement track at Aston, Birmingham, in a series of pro. races from 440 yards to 10 miles. Before leaving, he went around to his friends and neighbours, saying 'Goodbye'; and even went so far as to tell his father he felt he would never sleep in his own bed again. Will Jordan later told a reporter on *The Hub* that 'Harris had a curious foreboding that he would meet with another serious accident'.

It is a curious coincidence that both Bert's serious crashes occurred at Eastertime.

(He had suffered spills, of course, including one heavy 'wallop' on his last visit to France; but these were the ordinary type of 'bumps' that trackmen expect as part of the game).

Jordan told *The Hub* reporter, 'Bert raced at the Wood Green track without a tinge of nervousness; but when we reached home again a terrible sense of evil came over him and he could neither train nor rest. Even in his own home he didn't feel safe in his own bedroom'. Bert had indeed, ridden well at Wood Green the week before Easter, and one of his victims in the racing included Charley Barden, the Catford C.C. professional. Barden, a six-footer and the son of that same James Barden who had pioneered the cement-surfaced tracks in this country and abroad, was the same age as Bert, and had been a clubmate of his in the old Kensal Rise days. Barden had left the Poly in 1893, to join the Catford.

(Trackmen in the nineties were mostly all-rounders; specialists were the exception rather than the rule, as nowadays. Barden, for instance, was holder of the World 10 miles Record, but was still enough of a sprinter to take 2nd place in the World Professional Sprint Championships of 1896 and 1897. And Bert Harris, as we have seen, was equally at home at 440 yards or 10 miles).

The new Aston track had been built on the site of an older previous track – on which latter Bert had competed with Alf Edwards in their Amateur days – and was claimed to be 'the most modern track in Europe'. The *Sport and Play* newspaper proprietors were the lessees, and the rebuilding job, completed in 1896 had cost over £20,000. The straights were 110 yards long; the curved bankings 110 yards each, and 8ft. 6in. high. The backstraight was 24ft. wide, and the homestraight 28 feet. The main stand and pavilion was 450ft. long.

In later years the ground was sold to the Aston Villa Football Club, but cycle-racing was carried on until the outbreak of the Kaiser's War. The Aston track was finally demolished in 1920, to improve spectator accommodation for the Football Club; later a new cycle track was built in Birmingham to replace it. This is still in use today; it is of course Salford Park, the present $\frac{1}{4}$ mile circuit. The Aston site is today known as Villa Park; but in Bert's time the track was only one of a large collection of amusements and sideshows in a Sports Centre known as the 'Aston Lower Grounds.'

(The nearest approach to this Centre is perhaps the present-day Wicksteed Park at Kettering, with its Boating Pool, Fairground, $\frac{1}{4}$ mile Cycle Track, etc. – although the Southampton track is also set in similar surroundings).

At Aston, Easter Monday, 1897, Bert Harris was in fine form, and got 2nd in the Final of the $\frac{1}{4}$ mile handicap, despite puncturing in the last 80 yards. He walked over to the Dressing Rooms, lamenting the puncture, which meant 'standing down' from the main event, the 10 miles. However, a Birmingham amateur competitor, 'Fred' Pugh, offered his front wheel to Harris. It was a 28 x $1\frac{1}{4}$ 'Jointless' hollow steel rim, shod with a 'Palmer' tubular. Bert accepted the wheel with the remark, 'that looks a tidy wheel'.

(Pugh was later on the staff of the Rudge Cycle Company; his father was the actual patentee of the 'Jointless' Rim).

The fatal race commenced. After about 4 miles had been covered, Bert, following close on the wheel of London rider Ben Fisher, was seen to fall heavily. He struck the cement with the right side of his head. (Crash-helmets were unknown in those days even for motor-paced events). The field was travelling at about 27 m.p.h. at the time, and another rider fell on Harris. Fisher, despite a violent wobble, kept upright. Fred Chinn and Charley Barden, behind Harris, switched down on to the grass to avoid the fallen riders.

When the helpers reached Bert, he was unconscious; bleeding from a wound above the right ear, and also from the ear itself. He 'came to' for a few seconds, when the ambulance men took him away on a stretcher; and his friend Will Jordan, taking his hand, implored him, 'Come, Bert; pull yourself together a bit.'

Bert replied, 'Oh, Will, I am beat'.

He was taken to Birmingham General Hospital. He awoke briefly in hospital to say to his father, 'I am beaten this time'. (His father had rushed back from Cardiff, after Will Jordan telegraphed the sad news). Bert died at 5.20 a.m. on Wednesday, 21st April, 1897, in the presence of his father and sisters.

According to Mr Bennett, Resident Surgical Officer in the B.G.H. at that time, Bert died from 'Concussion of the brain and a fracture of the base of the skull'.

Meantime, the crash had become a topic of more than local interest.

The *Birmingham Daily Mail* reporter claimed that the wheel lent to Harris had a flaw in it, and 'the owner having ridden it for hundreds of miles, attached no importance to what unfortunately proved to be the source of weakness'.

He further suggested that the Professional Racing, being of a faster pace and fiercer nature than Pugh (the wheel's owner) was accustomed to in his Amateur events, therefore imposed a greater strain on the wheel; and that this extra strain while rounding the steep bankings of the new track, had caused the collapse of the wheel. He also quoted a witness as saying that Harris didn't touch anyone, and wasn't touched by anyone, when the crash occurred.

The Editorial in the same 'paper commented, 'There can be little doubt that the smash-up, caused by the buckling of the front wheel, was due to the cutting-down of the weight to the last ounce. These racing cycles are wonderfully strong, considering their web-like structure, but the point of perilous lightness is often too nearly approached'.

(An armchair critic, if ever there was one! Harris's trackiron – see Chapter 5 – was heavier than most track machines of the period, being $22\frac{1}{2}$ lbs. against the 21 lbs. of the 'Buckingham', 18 lbs. of the 'Demon', and the 19 lbs. of the 'Nelson').

The 'Jointless' Rim was very light gauge, and liable to dent easily; such dents were, of course, only superficial damage, and disregarded by the actual riders.

However, the newspaper critics, with their statements, had upset the makers of the 'Jointless', who commissioned solicitor T Tyler to attend the inquest on their behalf.

The inquest took place on Friday, 23rd April, at Birmingham Coroner's Court.

The rim, however, was vindicated when the elder Harris, on being handed the buckled wheel in court, declared the rim to be 'sound and well made. I don't think the crash was the fault of the rim'.

A juryman (evidently a cyclist) stated that he used the same type of rim himself, with no trouble; and that he weighed 13 stone, 7 lbs. as against the 10 stone, 4 lbs. of Harris.

Fred Chinn, in evidence, stated that he saw Harris touch Fisher's wheel, and wrench his 'bars in an effort to get away. Then came the crash.

According to Mr. Allcroft, a Leicester man and a great fan of Bert's all those years ago, local opinion insisted that Bert was 'bored' and 'bumped' by his rivals in this race . . . given what we would call these days 'a rough ride'.

It certainly sounds very strange, that any professional racing man of Harris's undoubted 'class' and international experience, would try such a novice manoeuvre as to 'pull away' from a touched wheel. Even the veriest novice knows enough to 'lay hard' on to a 'touched wheel'.

However, Bert's father may have touched on the truth in his evidence, and perhaps indicated the cause. He stated that the new (and bigger) gear of 92in. would tend to upset the rider's judgment, owing to the higher rate of speed coupled with a slower rate of pedalling. Still other witnesses were of the opinion that Fisher 'kicked back' to slow down. This of course is a possibility, as there was a lap prize in the 'ten', and riders would tend to 'ease' after each sprint for the lap line.

The funeral of Harris was held in bright sunny weather, and tens of thousands of people crowded the streets to pay a last tribute to Bert. Hundreds of wreaths filled the first two hearses, two of the floral tributes being from 'The Polytechnic Boys' – ('In Memory'), and Alf Edwards – who wrote on his card, 'To my dear old comrade in many a struggle'. Another wreath was from the Catford C.C. (Barden's Club).

Alf and Bert had been, as the *Poly C.C. Gazette'* put it, 'bosom friends'; and Alf never raced again after the 1897 season.

Bert Harris was 23 years old, at his death. He was always popular, optimistic, irrepressibly good-humoured, and a great Bike Rider; full of fun and always merry when racing.

He won over 300 prizes; an average of 40 a year for his racing career; plus thousands of pounds in cash, in his short time on this earth.

His grave, near the fence alongside University Road in Leicester, is near the site of the old Chapels in Welford Road Cemetery. (Two smooth lawns now occupy the site of the long-vanished Chapels). Harris's father died in February, 1924, at the age of 74, and is buried in the same grave as his wife and Bert.

Bearing in mind the class of rider that Bert was beating (such as Protin, Bourillon, Barden, to name but three) and his youth (only 23 at his death), it's not too much to assert that he probably would have attained World Championship honours if he'd not been snatched away from life so early. It wasn't until 1936 that the N.C.U. made crash-helmets compulsory for track-racing in this country.

CHAPTER TEN

LINKS

THE MODERN ADMIRER OF HARRIS can still find many links with Bert, as well as his grave. The *Aylestone Road Sports Ground* is now the County Cricket Ground of Leicestershire. A stretch of the original cinder-track, on which so many exciting races took place, is still used as a footpath along the Milligan Road side of the ground, although the surface is very rough now, of course.

Similarly, part of the home straight of the old Aston Track is still walked on by grandstand customers at Villa Park.

Harris's house at 4, Portsmouth Road, Leicester, is now a Coal and Paraffin Fuel Depot. The front room 'bursting with prizes and trophies' to quote the 1897 *Leicester Daily Post* reporter, is now a Showroom-cum-Office. The Kennington Oval is used solely for cricket these days; the Surrey B.C. is defunct.

Paddington, Herne Hill, and Fallowfield tracks are still very much used, but the Wood Green, Kensal Rise, Crystal Palace, Catford and Bristol tracks have vanished. Part of the old St Albans track is still visible in Clarence Park, not far from the present-day grasstrack. The remains of the old wood battens surface of Herne Hill are doing duty as fencing at the rear of the Stands. Cardiff track has been rebuilt into what my old friend Arie Van Vliet (ex-World Champion, both Amateur and Pro.) declared 'One of the best outdoor tracks in Europe'.

Holy Trinity Church is still a very active force for good, and many lay missionaries have been supplied by its congregation. The School, however, is almost derelict, although a local C.T.C. Section has made use of it as a Clubroom.

The *'Bert Harris' Trophy* is awarded annually to the winner of the Poly C.C. Midland Section 5 miles track Championship; the event being open to all members of the Club, whether members of the Midland Section or not. Leicester rider Bart Archer won it in 1963 on the Kettering track.

The Poly Club's Midland Section of the 'nineties, which included Bert Harris, Ernie Leitch, C W Schafer, W Griffiths, Teddy Young, Herbert Synyer, and many other 'big' names of Victorian Cycling, has of course been replaced by successive generations. The author is the current Section Secretary, and the Polytechnic C.C. Midlands Section's riders and officials are a very active cycling force.

(In 1962 and 1963 for instance, Johnson, Archer and Whitfield collected B.C.F. National Championship medals riding for Midland Section Polytechnic; in the same two years Johnson, Burns, Archer, McCarthy, and Whitfield collected B.C.F. Division Championship medals; in the same two years Polytechnic Club trophies were won by Archer, Hargreaves and Whitfield).

Some of *Bert's clubmate-contemporaries* are still alive today, including Alec Watson, who is over 90 and lives at Hastings; 'Taffy' Davies, 91, living at Sunningdale; and 91-year-old George Apsey.

Will Jordan's house, together with all the houses in the blocks between Mill Street and Regent Road, has been demolished. James Street is no longer on the local maps, and is indicated only by an un-named strip of asphalt.

The site of *Jordan's house,* on the corner of James Street and Welford Road, is now occupied by a Carpark Attendant's hut.

The Polytechnic Institute at 309, Regent Street, London, W.1., has been extensively renovated several times since Bert's day; his name is still to be seen in the Cycling Club's committee-room, on the gold-lettered Roll of Honour of Club Champions. The Club's photograph Album, in the care of Wally Gray, is a delightful pictorial history of the Poly C.C., going back to 1878; it contains several photographs of Bert and his pals. In Bert's day, a sloped awning covered the entrance to the Poly; a statue of

Britannia adorned the roof; and a network of rope nets and ladders surmounted the gymnasium, reaching from the gallery rails to the roof. (These have vanished, and two giant Trampolines now occupy the Gym for those who feel air-minded). The Refreshment Room of those days, is the Restaurant of nowadays – prices a little different, of course! The swimming-bath was very much as we see it today. The Cyclists' Room contained what appear to be the identical Secretary's Desk and Reading Table, that are there today. A picture from the 1896 Polytechnic Institute Magazine depicts the Cyclists' Room as also containing armchairs and reading-lamps; and framed pictures adorning the walls.

The place was known officially then, as the 'Polytechnic Young Men's Christian Institute'. (The Young Women's Branch in Langham Place was opened in 1888).

The Poly building cost Quintin Hogg £60,000; but the City Commissioners started to help financially in 1890. The word 'Polytechnic' passed into the language; and since those days, hundreds of local 'Polytechnics' have appeared all over Britain. But THE Polytechnic always means Regent Street. Quintin Hogg was president of the Poly C.C., rode a bicycle and was quite definitely in the hearts of the racing boys of Bert's day.

The current *Club President* and grandson of Quintin Hogg, Lord Hailsham, can also match his forbear by (a) riding a bicycle; and (b) claiming the affection of all ranks of the Club.

Australia still has strong links with the Poly C.C., with Poly Professionals Don Burgess and Peter Brotherton surrently performing in top class track racing 'Down under'. Peter Smith and Brian Johnson, two Poly Amateurs, are also in Australia currently racing in track events. (1962). Roger Whitfield, Leicester rider and Polytechnic C.C. 1962 Junior Champion, carried the coincidence still further by winning a Bronze Medal in the 1962 Empire Games in Perth, Australia.

The Belgrave Road Railway Station, built in 1883, and used by Bert for many of his racing trips, was closed in 1963 under the Beeching Plan.

The 'Jointless Rim' Company was eventually 'bought out' by Palmer's, and to this day Palmer rims are marked 'Jointless' and made in different fashion to the 'Dunlop'. The latter are cut from spirals of shaped steel, and joined by welding. This sometimes results in a 'flat' which is very annoying to wheelbuilders.

CHAPTER ELEVEN

COMMENTS

I HAVE COLLECTED A FEW COMMENTS by relevant personalities, that may be of background interest to the Harris story.

A E Davies, Polytechnic C.C., ex-President of the Fellowship of Old Time Cyclists, and holder of the N.C.U. Gold Badge of Honour, had this to say: 'The passing of Bert is a sad story, and I should say his first accident must have had a greater effect on him than one would imagine. I am of the opinion that Harris was not quite clear mentally at the time; and the damage to the Jointless Rim was caused by the crash alone. I had a lot of these Jointless Rims go through my hands' (Taffy was in the manufacturing side of cycling besides being a racing cyclist); 'although it was so light, the 'Jointless' was very strong, but liable to dent on the sides'.

Walter Groves, Editor of *Cycling* and Editor of the *Polytechnic C.C. Gazette,* writing in 1899, had this to say of Bert Harris: 'One of our most enthusiastic racers, and a most consistent prize-winner throughout his career. His good sportsmanship was never questioned. His death was a great blow to the club'.

The Hub weekly cycling newspaper, of 22nd May, 1897, reminiscing about Bert Harris, stated that: 'At the time when he was at the zenith of his fame, he was earning more money than any other professional of the day'.

Charley Barden, Catford C.C. World-Class rider, who died in Leicester in November, 1962, was of the opinion that a 'chop' had been fixed by some of the riders; and in fact, made himself unpopular with those he suspected, by being rather blunt in his comments. Charley was always noted for his honesty and outspoken manner.

John Edlin, currently Churchwarden at St Mary de Castro Church in Leicester, and a relative of the Walter Edlin who made the first special frames for Dunlop, recalls his father's stories of racing on the Belgrave Road track on an 'Ordinary', and later performances on the Aylestone Road track on a 'Safety'. Later, John's father opened a Bike Shop in Conduit Street, Leicester, and later still, a Branch Shop in Infirmary Square.

My own theory of the crash is that the wheel was put in, in a hurry; the adjusting cone may have been put on the right-hand side instead of the left, in the forks. This would cause the cones to lock up and thus take Harris's steering away. I just can't get Chinn's statement about 'wrenching the 'bars', to conicide with Harris's experience and knowledge of riding technique. Alternatively, the tracknuts may not have been tightened properly, or even 'stripped'. In any event, the feeling remains that if Bert hadn't punctured, and had been using his own wheel, the crash would not have occurred.

'Taffy' Davies again : 'The early British professional rider was not considered 'persona grata', and until the early 'nineties only a few towns, such as Leicester and Wolverhampton, would promote racing for them. When France became 'Tom Tiddler's Ground' in the 1894-8 period, many of my Poly club-mates joined in the 'Scoop-up' and the tone of the pro's improved. Later, the track went *all* pro., with the 'Chain Matches' (see *'The Charley Barden Story',* by R Swann – author), the 'Catford Gold Vase', and other classic pro. events', (When 'Taffy' was a Schoolboy at Stafford, he recalls seeing Robb, Howell, and English out training for Wolverhampton's pro. meets).

Walter Phillips, 'Humber' works manager in Bert Harris's time, writing in 1920, spoke of the N.C.U's early disinterest in professionalism, and recalled that the first pro. races were promoted in Manchester.

Then the landlord of the 'Molineaux Arms' in Wolverhampton encouraged pro-racing in a field behind the 'pub'. This developed until the 'Molineaux Grounds' became the scene of some famous

COMMENTS

battles between Robb, Howell, England and Phillips himself. (The 'Molineaux Grounds' are nowadays known as the H.Q. of the 'Wolves' Football Club).

Big purses were put up, huge crowds and large entries were the rule. This was in the '70's, when the 'Ordinary' was taking over from the 'Boneshakers'. By the early 80's, however, the centre of Pro. Bike-racing was Leicester. Phillips referred to Leicester as 'the other town which encouraged professional racing'.

The Amateur Clubs in Leicester included the Leicester B.C., the Syston and Belgrave Clubs, and a couple of 'Business Houses' clubs. (Author's note: None of these has survived; the oldest Leicester-only club of modern times being the Leicestership R.C., formed in 1908 from the remnants of the Syston and Belgrave clubs). In addition there were, in Harris's time (and still are), sections of the Poly C.C. and of the C.T.C.

Doctor Moss and Doctor Kind, in their fight against the apathy of Leicester's powers-that-be in the Typhoid Scare of the early 1960's, have underlined the continued unhygienic outlook of Leicester, with the Rivers Soar and Washbrook in a 'foul condition' and 'an absolute disgrace', according to letters in the *Leicester Mercury* of 1963. In fact, the River Soar is jocularly mispronounced 'Sewer' by Leicester people of 1963!

The pneumatic tyre (see Chap. 3), 'which has created such a sensation in the cycling world', said *The Graphic* of October 4th, 1890, 'may be, after all, not a novelty. Someone has discovered an old patent, taken out in 1845, for an almost identical invention'. This refers, of course, to the Thomson patent. (*The Graphic* also comments on a new three-quarter mile record by Ernie Leitch of the Polytechnic).

Brian Johnson, present-day Poly rider performing so well in Australia (1962-3), after reading what he calls 'the evidence', had this to say: 'It's quite obvious that Harris's fear was due to a very real knowledge; in other words, he'd been threatened with a 'chop' by another rider or riders'. And, bearing in mind the 'shady, dishonest, and vicious characters who indulge in professional cycle racing', as Lacy Hillier put it, there may be some truth in Johnson's idea. One writer in *The Hub* of 1897, declared that 'the fixing of races, and the dishonest practices that are looked on as normal procedure among certain classes of professionals, would hardly be believed'. (The betting evil, plus the large cash prizes, were naturally good reason for 'keen competition').

And, of course, there is the example of the Welshman James, plus the conflicting evidence (some of it unreal, to say the least), of the eye-witnesses of the Aston crash.

EPILOGUE

SINCE THIS BOOK WAS FIRST PUBLISHED in 1964, Leicester now has its own World-class Velodrome, on the site of the grasstrack on which the Author promoted the Leicester Track League meetings of the early 1960's. And after the long gap from 1881, once again the World Championships have been held in Leicester (1970).

APPENDIX

THERE IS A LITTLE CONFUSION over the exact site of the Aylestone Road grounds; but although the Cricket Club now refer to the ground as the 'Grace Road' grounds, and the present W. boundary is not in contact with Aylestone Road, in Harris's day the present-day Park Hill Drive did not exist, and the ground did in fact extend to the Aylestone Road.

Later, the Cricket Club purchased ground further up the Aylestone Road, near the junction of Ayleston Road and Saffron Lane. This was in 1901, and to obtain a sufficiently large playing-space, part of the ancient earthworks known as the Raw Dyke, were levelled.

By this time the old ground's contact with Aylestone Road had disappeared, with its shrinking in size owing to the building of houses and new roads. To differentiate between the two Sports Grounds, the new ground was named the 'Aylestone Road' ground, and the old ground re-named 'Grace Road'.

The Grace Road ground was originally built as a pleasure and recreational area; twelve acres specially prepared for cricket, surrounded by cycling and running tracks; a residential hotel was built and the total cost of the venture was about £40,000. The grounds were opened in 1878, but cycle-racing was confined to local local events until the closing of the Belgrave Road ground in 1884. Then the Aylestone Road ground became the new centre of cycle-racing in Leicester.

The residential hotel (still there) was managed by ex-Leicester County Cricket star Pougher, until a few years ago, when he died. A collection of cycling, athletic, and cricketing photographs adorned the walls of the public bar in those days. Pougher's

APPENDIX

widow is still living, and resides at Scaptoft, a few miles outside Leicester. E Snow, writing in 1960, said that the ground's correct name was the 'Aylestone Ground', and that it was never named as 'Aylestone Road'; however, the Leicester newspapers, and record-books, N.C.U. lists, etc., of the period, all refer to it as the 'Aylestone Road Ground'.

Groundsmen for the Harris period were:

J Garner (1884-9); W Cooke (1890-1);

G Panter (1892); and E Horne (1893-1901).

After this book was written, came the news of the death of A E ('Taffy') Davies – the source of much of my information on the life and times of Bert Harris. I hope to write the story of 'Taffy's' life, in the not-too-distant future.